T0149788

# NOMADIC PRESS

## OAKLAND

111 FAIRMONT AVENUE
OAKLAND, CA 94611

## BROOKLYN

475 KENT AVENUE #302
BROOKLYN, NY 11249

WWW.NOMADICPRESS.ORG

## MASTHEAD

FOUNDING PUBLISHER
J. K. FOWLER

ASSOCIATE EDITOR
MICHAELA MULLIN

EDITOR
BRENNAN DEFRISCO

DESIGN
JEVOHN TYLER NEWSOME

## MISSION STATEMENT

Through publications, events, and active community participation, Nomadic Press collectively weaves together platforms for intentionally marginalized voices to take their rightful place within the world of the written and spoken word. Through our limited means, we are simply attempting to help right the centuries' old violence and silencing that should never have occurred in the first place and build alliances and community partnerships with others who share a collective vision for a future far better than today.

## INVITATIONS

Nomadic Press wholeheartedly accepts invitations to read your work during our open reading period every year. To learn more or to extend an invitation, please visit: www.nomadicpress.org/invitations

## DISTRIBUTION

Orders by teachers, libraries, trade bookstores, or wholesalers:

Nomadic Press Distribution
orders@nomadicpress.org
(510) 500-5162
nomadicpress.org/store

Small Press Distribution
spd@spdbooks.org
(510) 524-1668 / (800) 869-7553

This book was made possible by a loving community of chosen family and friends, old and new.

For author questions or to book a reading at your bookstore, university/school, or alternative establishment, please send an email to info@nomadicpress.org.

Cover art: Arthur Johnstone

Published by Nomadic Press, 111 Fairmount Avenue, Oakland, California 94611

First printing, 2022

Library of Congress Cataloging-in-Publication Data

Title: *Hello Joy*
p. cm.
Summary: *Hello Joy* is a blissful dive into the current of sorrow and ecstasy which make up the cycles of our depression. This collection is an ode to all the simple moments of pleasure that pull us back to the shoreline, that despite our surmounting darkness will always and inevitably find our joy again.

[1. POETRY / Subjects & Themes / Healing. 2. POETRY / Subjects & Themes / Mental Health. 3. POETRY / American / General.]
I. III. Title.

LIBRARY OF CONGRESS CONTROL NUMBER: 2021949442

ISBN: 978-1-955239-17-2

# HELLO JOY

JARVIS SUBIA

# HELLO JOY

## JARVIS SUBIA

**NOMADIC
PRESS**

# CONTENTS

reading guide

# NOTES FROM THE GARDEN

Today, I trim the tomatoes,
seed the cucumbers, Fertilize the roses,
I am preparing for the growth
Summer brings

Before October's slow wilting.
Funny how we call it fall
A month of remembering
Death before the season
We experience it the most.

During the cold months
I am mostly composting
Between sleep cycles,
Depression robs the body
Of its energy nutrient.

Most days, I forget to eat
And wither by 4 pm
Refuse to leave my bed
For anything less than warming

I'm an educator who plants
A garden but never tends to myself.
Teaches the youth a workshop
On self-care and neglects
To fill my body with water.

Fact:
plants will gain more foliage
During the winter;
they will not flower or Fruit: it is okay
To spend seasons
In preparation instead of growth,
To spend years buried under a rock
Before you have a name for this illness
Before anxiety severs your friendships
And the panic attacks find you,
In a car / a party / an art show.

Fact: some trees won't experience
Any growth for the first few years
I am approaching my first anniversary
Of being in committed therapy
Because I found the community clinic

It took that long for me to accept
Health is greater than
The reach of burning kush.
It's taken me even longer
To begin treating the sadness
With things that don't grow
From the soil. My psychiatrist
Tells me to swallow two small seeds
Per day and watch what takes root

Inside me
Mental health is an alchemy
Between medicine and remedy
Between good company and
My tongue hesitating over
The consents of the stigma label

My therapist tells me
I don't need to be able to pronounce
the name, just swallow, and I do.
I don't tell people I grow organic,
Mostly because I use Miracle Grow,

But also because I've been taught
To believe, I don't know how to use
The tools that have been gifted to me
Well enough

but I have learned to bury
Some bad habits,
Put them into the garden,
Hope they don't grow back,
And when they do,
I consider that a miracle.

# AN ODE TO FACIAL HAIR AND ELEGY TO THE MAN I WAS

My beard / Hairy

My beard / Thick in all the right places

My beard / A grizzly bear

       Consumed by a forest of black redwoods

My beard / Yet to offer itself as lumbar

My beard / Every beard in "300 Spartan"

       Each thread, an extended foot

       Aimed at the chest of anyone questioning

       Its color, shouting

       THIS! ISN'T! ROGAINE!


My beard / Gets asked

       Do you want to go camping?

       Or hunting?

       Or hiking?

       Or start a fire?

       Or start a fist fight?

       Or take this shot?

       Or get sloppy drunk?

       Do you want to forget her name?

       And his name? (definitely his name)

       And your name too?

My beard / Passing for masculinity
        Allowing everyone to still assume it of me.


My beard / Becoming
        A choir whistling Dixie to the same old tune
        Of each generation teaching it's sons
        How to be like their fathers.


My beard / A hymn I'm still learning
        To live in, clasped hands dug into my chin
        Praying to the god I see in men
        To let me see god in myself.


My beard / Resilience
        When I feel cut down and struggling
        To unbox my binary into the spectrum
        A guard against people who feel the need
        To redefine my vision of masculinity
        As if any action could lift this shroud and
        Revile someone other than myself


My beard / an experience that is owning sexuality

Tucked tightly inside questioning manhood

Like the way all my gender labeled products
Sit daintily in the shower
The coconut oil,
The pink silky smooth
Head and Shoulders,
Mens navy blue deep clean conditioner,
Red Spice body gel
        The one with a picture of two ungendered wolves on the
front
Post shower cucumber peel, sandalwood beard oil

The most manly I feel is
        When my eyebrows are plucked and shaped
Because serving face is the cleanest revolt

My youth comprised of convincing
The boys of my biology
That I am not hiding

Behind what they see,
when what they see
Is not who I am,
when who I am
only wants to be seen /
           Wants to be accepted.

I had watched my peers bully
The queer men I secretly admired
Do you know what it's like
To watch your own closeting? /
           To watch all your courage sink
           Back into yourself

The most boyish thing I've become
Is still learning to defend
The parts of myself which define me

A desire to grow but never change
My desire to speak, Instead listen to the voices
Heckling from behind the mirror
That this swallowed face

Isn't as it should be

Salvaged masculinity, falling
In line with internalized homophobia
Knowing how effeminate queer men /
        Who are literary men
Threaten everything within
This harmful bubble
Praise be the needle-bearer

Most days /
        Masculinity feels like plummeting
        The whole way down, wondering
        If I could be male /
                not broken?
        If this vulnerable ego could live /
                Without the mask, and
        Allow myself the birthright of being
        As queer or feminine as I want to be
        And calling that manhood.

My beard / Not about why

       I choose to be the person under it

       But about how all of it is me.

# ODE TO CHEESE

## YO! GOOEY!
### I SEE YOU THERE
SLICK AND SLIDING OFF THE TOP
## OF MY PEPPERONI PIZZA
### BURSTING LIKE THRONGS
## FROM THE CRUST AND
I SHOULD POINT OUT THAT PIZZA
## WITHOUT THE CHEESE
## IS JUST A SAD TACO
WITH REALLY BLAND SALSA OR
A CRACKER AND SALAMI
## DRYING OUT
ALL THE SALIVA IN MY MOUTH,
## SOMETIMES,
I WAKE IN THE MIDDLE OF THE NIGHT
FROM ONE OF THOSE GLISTENING FANTASIES,
### THE ONE WHERE THE PEOPLE
## FROM INSTAGRAM VIDEOS
WALK OVER TO A HEAD SIZE ROUND OF GOUDA
HANGING OVER TEH GOLDEN AND ASH WHITE
OF MESQUITE, CURTAIN OF BROWNING DAIRY
### HANGING LIKE A WATERFALL OR
### ADELE'S VOICE OR MAYBE

I JUST HEAR BOTH, BUT THEN, SLIDES
IT'S OOZING AND EBBING INTO A LARGE BOWL
AND BRING IT OVER
TO THE OIL SLICK OF
A CUSTOMER'S EYES WAITING FOR
THE CHEESE TO WASH
OVER THEIR PLATE
OF POTATOES OR RIBEYE STEAK
EXCEPT THE STEAK IS ME.
I WANT TO BATHE IN CHEDDAR
AND MONEY
BUT MOSTLY IT'S RICHNESS
LIKE AIN'T NO
DADDY SEXIER THAN
CHESTER CHEESE,
LIKE SOMETIMES, IN MY MIND
I PINCH UP THE
CORNER OF THE BAG AND
INSTEAD OF A FEW

CRUMBS FALLING
INTO MY MOUTH
GUNS MAKING IT RAIN,
OVER THE LOW
RASP OF HIS VOICE WHISPERING
"IT AINT EASY BEIN' CHEESEY,"
SOMETIMES, I SIT BACK AND WISH
MY HAIR WAS MADE
OUT OF STRING CHEESE,
LIKE THE LOVE CHILD
OF GANDALF
AND A PLATE OF CARNE ASADA FRIES
SO WHEN PEOPLE TELL ME
HOW GOOD I SMELL OR HOW
PRETTY I LOOK
I CAN SAY
I GOT IT FROM MY MAMA.
AND TO CLARIFY
ANYTIME SOMEBODY CALLS ME

# A SNACK
WHAT THEY MEAN IS A CHEEZE-IT,
WHAT THEY MEAN IS I'M AGED
## AND IT TOOK ME A
LONG TIME TO GET HERE
TO PALATE MYSELF FOR YOUR
## CONSUMPTION.
I WANT TO BE TOASTED AND SAUCY AND
## DRIPPING
INTO YOUR THOUGHTS

# ETYMOLOGY

The first time I'd ever met somebody who shared my name. I was already 22 years old into this solitary epithetless life. His name was Jarvis, he was 5 years old, and to nobody's surprise was kind of freaked out that this grown-ass-man was so excited to meet him. This thought passes my mind as the Peet's barista stares me down the barrel of her nose and with all the confidence of a white woman, selling fair-trade coffee from ethnic third world countries, slow drips out a more palatable title for my cup.

"You said Travis right?"

by now I've already lost count of the number of times someone has taken my name into their mouth and spit out the bones of who they want me to be. I am always dead in this scenario; there is no version of colonization where the mixed boy makes it out whole.

When asked of my names origin: My father tells me I was named after a star NCAA running back, most of my students tell me "Iron man", instead I think my grandmother has it closest, a woman who has never felt the need to sacrifice her tongue for this flag, sometimes mixes up Jarvis with the English word for *Ghar-bish* and sometimes call me basura and I have stopped correcting her because a quick google search will tell you that it is of Nordic: white: colonizer descent translating to "the servant spear," a name given to loyal warriors who serve the purpose of the empire.

More digging will lead to British surnames who sailed to my people's land on the backs of slave ships, and when I'm already branded with a conquistadors last name I often find myself asking who do I fight for?: whose service was I intended when stolen lineage bookends my identity?

They say in the beginning the ship sailed onto the rock then lost man names found people lost, names them improper, names their land his own, names this the beginning. Ya know, the act of naming is a kind of colonization, it says "you are now only what we call you." US history has a funny way of naming itself, calls genocide: manifest, enslavement: labor, calls Oligarchy: Democracy, post-racial: 13th amendment, lineage: how many of my ancestors learned to run or fight?

My grandfather Alea, who his wife calls Alejandro, and we call Alexander tells me he still has vivid memories as a boy of US Naval planes flying overhead towards Pearl Harbor: reminds me how this country turned a people marginal, our land: monetary: warzone: united, how they never wanted to name us until there was something worth taking: reminded of the duality in being both ethnic and American, both claimed and reclaiming, of the Brown Berets & Dolores Huerta & Emilio Zapata

& Lili'uokalani & Kamehameha & James Cook's head piked against ocean. We have called ourselves resistance for so long it runs in our blood.

My name is mine and I do not wish to give it back but I am learning to sharpen my edges and serve the people to fight for What. Is. Ours. to learn our names as our land no longer for your claiming.

# SCENARIOS IN WHICH I WOULD SAVE MY CATS

there's a tree and my calico --Maya-- is on the top
branch and the palm tree is on fire from molten lava  erupting
out from a ground fissure beneath it, which is now spewing
toxic gas. i would shimmy my way up that trunk like some sort
of lumberjack soccer mom, lumboccer-mom? *[work in progress]*
I'd make my way to the top with a water hose clenched between
my teeth.

an alley cat attempts to break into our house to snag some
Friskies, gets into a scuffle with Gigi ending with their claws
pressed tight against Gigi's throat. That mothafucka's getting
a squirt bottle to the face.

vacuum cleaners. all day.

hawks. i don't really know how i'm going to fight a hawk but
we'll figure it out when we get there.

It's easier to figure out ways i could save my cat than say my cat
saved me. to admit some days depression crashes so hard on my
shore there is only enough energy to coil my way into bed.

sadness, is a sneaky nightcrawler knows just the right triggers to cue an entrance in any public setting. knots a furball in my chest out of the days regrets. thinking about what others are thinking about me which they're probably not thinking about, that love is a gift i only get to watch be received, or how all my irrational fears will come true tonight.

like cats, my sadness thinks the answer is food. that satisfaction is found at a bowl's pit or a plate's rind or maybe mistakes dishes for voided hearts or just sees plates as the appropriation of skin to mouth, the reason i will not touch anyone in fear of colonizing the people i love, a selfish midas i've become. hungry for whoever can feed my empty at the cost of their own consumption.

my depression is rooted in my fear of receiving love or maybe i've inherited too much space for it or maybe there's so much not-joy inside me but --like cats-- i'm just trying to be cool about it. canceling plans with a friend translates to "i don't know where to fit you next to all this empty emotion. A home built of all the times i've apologised for myself."

i lied. i saved the cat before it saved me. there was not a fire or car chase or semi-automatic gun shootout in a inner-city warehouse. just the basin of a boy and a kitten that found its way to his porcelain heart.

# SCENARIOS IN WHICH MY CAT SAVES ME

On my worst days,
all I want is someone
to run their hands
through my hair
tell me things
are going to be
okay, that the world
will not end today,
that i will move forward
like a feline through the tall grass
looking for the other side.
on my worst days, my cat
has a habit of pressing
their head into my hand
wanting me to scratch
behind the ear, asking
if everything
is going to be
okay.

# A GUIDE FOR BREAKING THROUGH THE NIGHT INTO THE MORNING

a flower knows it's time to wake
when the light offers a feast
glowing as the thin lake brushed
over each leaf and falling
to puddle the ripe soil underneath
thick with the breakdown
your environment should provide
all your needs to build itself
my family knows it sunday
when Otis Redding spills from stereo
and seeds home in everyone's chest
when I am in the garden i am singing
Whitney or Gloria
i wipe my brow with the same
muddy hand i grab the imaginary mic
i've become mad with mystery
in discovering what becomes of each
new room i build for myself
misshapen temple
abandoned holy land
of dirty and little

hold me here
with a shovel and watering can
ready to dig my hands
up through the clay
into daylight

# DANCING AT THE GAY BAR

I am a bath of light /
Sunburst in full bloom /
A cascading 2 step.
I shimmy like a star
Sliding off its silk
Horizon, into midnight /
Wet-dream slip-n-slide /
Worthy of all $10 entry and $40
On drinks that you flirted with
The half-naked bartender to get /
The split drink running
On the painted hardwood,
Well, are you?
Did you know I was coming?
Ready to backup all this ass,
Shaken, the thread spooling
Inside your jeans.

Yet masc-boy-wallflower,
Gets stared at
Like I don't belong here.
Like I didn't flirt with the same

Bartender for drinks.
Like cis-male presenting ain't
Mean I don't know how

To shake it,
Like pansexual boy ain't
Confused, he's just drunk
On all this wanting.
How the salt on neck
Taste the same either way,
Like I aint top/ bottom/
Reverse/ dom/ sub/
All the same,
Like passing didn't mean
All my old friends let me
Walk out of the closet alone
Then became the lint on this fit,
Like I didn't brush my
Shoulder lean with it pop with it
Thizz face Bernie,
Like I still brought the whole hood
Who didn't come with me

To the club tonight,
Like I aint the Hyphy-ist rainbow
In the bay, boi!
Like my thighs and hips and back
Ain't sore from all this work,
So come get it

Come tell me how my sexuality
Still makes you uncomfortable,
Like it hasn't even been 2 years
Since a man,
Who wears my pronouns
Like a bad relationship
With his father,
Walked into the sanctuary
Of Pulse nightclub
And asks a room full
Of queer fireworks
To bend at the bullet.

It reminds me how we are still
Safe nowhere

Not even in the houses built by
The hands of people
Who suffered for
Our identity,
Remembering some have
Constructed entire religions out of
Wanting our bright faces
Ceaseless.

Masculinity feeling like
A costume I wear for safety,
A performance which
Manhood has become
The greatest theater for.
But ain't no man bold enough
To stop all this movement
Being proud of yourself
Is a praise dance
for our queer ancestors, who
Watch from the heavens
As their rainbow children
Thrive in gold and white light

So don't come in here acting like
You ain't trying to stare at the sun,
Like you didn't try to hold
All this heat in the eye,
I will sear you at the gaze,
Friction that blasphemous
Booty mouth you came here
Looking for.
And I dance through midnight
Till we have risen. And we will rise.
Watch us.

# THIS WILL BE THE YEAR

*after Martín Espada and Warsan Shire*

This will be the year of movement,
The year I learn to dance publicly
Like nobody's watching
The year of hips and cumbia
The year of percussion and  ceaseless heartbeat
The year I allow the music to consume me
Until I birth back as song.

This will be the year of travel,
The year I learn to leave
And return for what's not worth letting go
The year I learn rest
The year I learn cannabis as self-care
And self-indulgence,
The year I turn up, turn out, and turn in
This will be the year the Monarch gets live
Fluttering out the cocoon,
Better recognize an emperor in new clothes
So that you can see all that I am,
When bass breaks through the throat
And becomes soul.

This will be the year I ask for all my clothes back
 And give back all the people I've become clothing for.
This will be the year of friendship
And the different faces of love
The year I try a little tenderness
This will be the year I learn I need you
More than you need me
The year I live and let love.

This will be the year I open my heart and say,
"You are allowed to live here
Even if you choose not to stay"
The year I learn I cannot save you
If my own ship is sinking,
This is the year I continue to be reminded that
Jack could have survived the titanic
if he had known how violent his own heart could be.

This will be the year of passion and spring
This will be the year I learn to wear flowers
and bloom
This will be the year of Simone and Santana and -yoncé

Of Ocean and Mercury and Keys
This will be the year I learn to cut and scratch the record of my life
The year I remix and rebirth and revolution
This will be the year I learn my voice
As power and change,
As symbol and circumstance,
As my own name and gift.

The year I learn to become a student
then teacher then student again then all at once
The year I learn word-economy and not volume
This will be the year I learn to make more use
Of my ears than my mouth
The year I learn to hear you
Even when you're not speaking

The year I run wild
know what can never be tamed
become unbashful, unapologetic, unbroken

The year I forgive myself
And learn I didn't need to

This will be the year *I celebrate myself, I sing myself*
This will be the year I learn all the words
I've been searching for
This will be the year of becoming
The year you finally meet me
The year I will love you so, so much.

# AT DINNER

You say     your eyes are 2 mosaics to a chapel I long to pay in.
 I say, pfffff haha ummm     thank you?          You say          I want
to set up camp across from you   at the dinner table    and listen to
your voice creek through the silverware like a soft breeze bouncing
against pine                 and I say, whaaaaaaaa?     You say     I saw
you!     The lost night I gaze into the void and spotted you nooked
between cassiopeia and andromeda         waiting for a reason     And
I say   I'm sorry I don't have time    and you say words like, appreciate
and grateful                 and I am hastily checking my emails or for
the exits      and you say   maybe we could just grab a coffee    and I
am filling my calendar   as fast as my thumbs can type      and you say
sometimes the heart is a cracked vessel        sinking      as soon as its
set onto the water and you have to decide    if will you flee    or let it
consume you      and I say but who    is worth the downing?
and you say                      you are.

# SELENA

*after Janae Johnson*

*Ay ay ay, cómo me duele*
*Ay ay ay, cómo me duele*

Selena gone and made a cumbia
Your abuela can dance to
Selena prayer of the 1 gen,
ni aqui ni alla,
Queen of Tejano.

Selena went and learned Spanish
Then made Tex-Mex music
You forgot was born in America.
Selena gone birthed a movie which
In turn, birthed a J-Lo.

Selena went and got your man
Weeping on the couch
And the latinidad ain't cried so hard
During a movie since Richie
Caught a plane into the sunrise
And the country only mourned
The white men.

Selena went and put 5 albums
On the Billboard charts ¡No mames!
at the same damn time.

Selena sang her own funeral/love song
Because celebrating life after death
Is about as Mexican as it gets.

Selena went and became a history
Of remembering brown excellence
And thriving glory
Of longing potential,
And swelling cultural pride.
Feel that glistening
in the corner of your eye
See, Selena left you that.

# NOTES FROM THE GARDEN

Today I trim the tomatoes
Water the strawberries
Pickle the cucumbers
Vinegar and salt
Today I am preparing for a bounty
We planted a garden here
Where there was only clay
And rock and weed and dirt
As a child
My family was so poor
I never frolicked in the grass
But instead rolled in the mud
A seed will always do better
In the wet earth
How my need to sprout through
Is what always motivated me forward
Pass my peers lounging on a gifted lawn
Oh hair, how the income bracket is a tortoise
of time, and I will keep running
Until all my bones and inherited bones
become a shield. We bury our dead
Full well knowing one day

they will become a garden
Knowing full well that I dug my hands
Into the soil
And became my ancestor's wildest dream.
I build plant containers and buy compost
My grandfather & his father & his father &
His father all cut the sugarcane
in Hawaii, they forgot the Caribbean
Island they buried their fathers' bones in.
While my 6-year-old niece tells me
She does not own a memory
without foliage
And somewhere today
I pour the blue miracle
into a watering can
And prepare for spring.

# READING GUIDE

Hello Educators! First, I'd like to extend my deepest gratitude for wanting to bring the poems inside of Hello Joy into your classroom space. I have been a teaching artist in the Bay Area for the past 6 years, going into classrooms and teaching lessons just like the ones I'm providing here. I usually enter the classroom with the aim of introducing the students I work with to the poets I love so dearly. Though I usually become some consumed with teaching other poets works that I often neglect to bring in my own, which is why I am so honored you would do so. These small lessons are intended to be guides or outlines that can be nestled in your schedule for the day. Feel free to remix them or add your own seasons and spices, I believe education should be a collaborative experience. Thank you again and hope with these your students can reintroduce themselves to that spark of joy.

## Title: **This Will Be The Year**

## Check-in Question
*(to be answered in a large or small group)*

o   What is something you accomplished in the last year?

## Read
*(to be read aloud or watches)*

- o "This Will Be The Year" (p. 29)
- o Watch the poem on youtube: Jarvis Subia - *This is the Year*

## Optional
*(see these poems that inspired the piece as reference)*

- o Martin Espada - *Angels of Bread*
- o Warsan Shire - *The year of letting go...*

## Discussion
*(capture students responses on the board)*

- o What is a personal affirmation?
- o When you imagine the next year of your life what are some hopes you would want for yourself?
- o When you imagine the next year of your life what are some hopes others (friends, family, close people) might want for yourself?
- o What do you want to let go of over the next year?

## Prompt
*(A guided free-write students could take in any direction)*

**Just like the poem we just read, create a list poem. A list poem is a piece of writing where each line isn't necessarily connected to the one before it or the one after. They are just individual thoughts running in descending**

**order, like a grocery list or to-do list. Except in this list, you will manifest the hope your want for the next year of your life, feel free to reference your collective notes.**

If you need a starting line to borrow the one from the poem, "This will be the year..." use it as many times as you like. Happy writing!

## Share
I highly encourage to leave space for sharing at the end, call it an *Open Mic*

# Title: **Odes, the hypemen of poetry**

## Check-in Question
*(to be answered in a large or small group)*

o   How would you define hype?

## Read
*(to be read aloud or watches)*

o   "Ode to Cheese" (p. 11)

o   Watch the poem "An Ode to Facial Hair"

## Discussion
*(capture students responses on the board)*

o   What are foods do you consider absolutely delicious? Why?

- Tell me about a movie, TV show, song, or artist you can't get out of your head? Why?
- Who are some of your favorite people? Why?
- What is something or someone that deserves more hype?

## Prompt

*(A guided free-write students could take in any direction)*

**I often conder Odes to be the hype men of poetry. Their job is to make a topic look fantastic, amazing, unstoppable, and the absolute best. An ode is an expression of love and admiration of a person, a topic, an item, a place in time, etc... pretty much anything you think is incredible.**

In this prompt, you're going to pick one thing, possibly something from the discussion or an idea that came up after, and write a poem that speaks to how much you really enjoy it. This is meant to be a free write so take it where ever your heart desires.

Starting lines could be, "Let me tell you about..." or "One of my favorite things is..."

## Share

I highly encourage to leave space for sharing at the end, call it an *Open Mic*

# Title: **Story of Your Name**

## Check-in Question
*(to be answered in a large or small group)*

- Who is a character on a TV show or an artist with a unique name?
  Ex: jean michel basquiat

## Read
*(to be read aloud or watches)*

- "Etymology" (p.15)
- Watch a performance of the poem "Etymology" - "Etymology" @ WANPOETRY

## Discussion
*(capture students responses on the board)*

- What is a nickname you or someone in your family has?
- How did they get that name?
- Have you ever named a pet? How did you arrive at their name?
- What does it mean to be called a name you don't like? Like if someone was making fun of your or someone you know?

## Prompt
*(A guided free-write students could take in any direction)*

**Write about the story of your name or a nickname you received? How did you get it? Is there a deeper meaning to it? Do you like it?**

Alternatively, write about a time someone called you something other than your name. Whether it is a nickname, a cruel name, or something else. What happened? How did it make you feel? What do you wish your response was?

Starting lines could be, "Let me tell you about..." or "One of my favorite things is..."

## Share

I highly encourage to leave space for sharing at the end, call it an *Open Mic*

# Title: I Am...

## Check-in Question
*(to be answered in a large or small group)*

o    What's a good quality you enjoy in others?

## Read
*(to be read aloud or watches)*

o    "Dancing At The Gay Bar" (p. 24)

- Watch a performance of the poem "I will dance through midnight, till we have risen and we will rise"

## Discussion
*(capture students responses on the board)*

- What talents are in the room or what are you really good at?
- What nationalities, cultures, or races are in the room?
- What someone looks at you what don't they see?

## Prompt
*(A guided free-write students could take in any direction)*

**Write an "I Am" poem. A poem that states all the identities that makeup who you are. As you are writing this poem, consider ways you identify big and small. Are you an athlete or a singer or do you make the best PB&J sandwiches? Think of ways of hyping yourself too, tell us how you're the dopest in different ways (IE. "I am a bath of light...") Start each line or new thought with the phrase "I Am..."**

## Share

I highly encourage to leave space for sharing at the end, call it an *Open Mic*

## Jarvis Subia

Born and raised in San Jose's Seven Trees Neighborhood, Bay Area Spoken Word Poet Jarvis Subia is a Queer Latinx flower-loving Melenial devoted to performing poems from his heart to yours.

The 2019 Poetry Foundation and Crescendo Literary's Incubator Fellow, the recipient of the 2019 Silicon Valley Creates & Content Magazines Emerging Artist Award, a 2019 Multicultural Artists Leadership Institute (MALI) fellow, San José Poetry Slam's 2018 Grand Slam Champion, and has competed in 14 national and regional poetry slam. He has been a teaching artist throughout the Bay Area for the past 5 years. Jarvis is currently living in the Boston area attending the Harvard Graduate School of Education.

# OTHER WAYS TO SUPPORT NOMADIC PRESS' WRITERS

In 2020, two funds geared specifically toward supporting our writers were created: the **Nomadic Press Black Writers Fund** and the **Nomadic Press Emergency Fund**.

The former is a forever fund that puts money directly into the pockets of our Black writers. The latter provides dignity-centered emergency grants to any of our writers in need.

Please consider supporting these funds. You can also more generally support Nomadic Press by donating to our general fund via nomadicpress.org/donate and by continuing to buy our books. As always, thank you for your support!

Scan below for more information and/or to donate.
You can also donate at nomadicpress.org/store.